ST. MARY'S R.C. PRIMARY SCHOOL

GOING SHOPPING

PENNY MARSHALL

Macdonald

Jacket pictures

Front (main): A grocer's shop, 1950s
Front (small): A butcher's shop in Tower Hamlets, London, c. 1870
Back (top): Interior of a chemist's shop in Ipswich, Suffolk, c. 1880
Back (bottom): A general hardware shop, c. 1880

For John

First published in 1984 by
Macdonald & Co. (Publishers) Ltd
London and Sydney

© Macdonald & Co. (Publishers) Ltd 1984

ISBN 0 356 10143 6

Macdonald & Co. (Publishers) Ltd
Maxwell House
74 Worship Street
London EC2A 2EN

A BPCC PLC company

Printed by Purnell & Sons (Book Production) Ltd
Paulton, near Bristol, Avon

BRITISH LIBRARY CATALOGUING IN PUBLICATION DATA

Marshall, Penny
    Going shopping–(Camera as witness)
    1. Shopping–Great Britain–History–
Juvenile literature
    I. Title II. Series
    381'.1'0941   TX335

ISBN 0-356-10143-6

CREDITS

Aldus Archive: 5, 22
Aldus Archive/Tower Hamlets Library:
    front cover (inset)
Barnaby's Picture Library: 10(top), 36,
    37(bottom), 39(top)
BBC Hulton Picture Library: front
    cover, 21(bottom), 27(top)
Burnley District Library: 15,
    27(bottom)
Robin Bush, *Jeboult's Taunton* (1983): 7
Chertsey Museum: 24(top)
Clwyd Record Office: 26
Dorset Natural History and
    Archaeological Society: 25
Electricity Council: 39(bottom)
Mary Evans Picture Library: 13, 19, 20,
    23
Leicestershire Record Office: 16(top
    and bottom), 17(top), 18-19
Lincoln Library, Local Studies
    Collection: 34, 34-35, 35
Mansell Collection: back cover (bottom),
    17(bottom), 30, 32(top)
National Magazine Company Ltd:
    24(bottom), 39(centre)
Northampton Central Library: 29(top)
Oxfordshire County Council:
    29(bottom)
Plymouth City Museum: 12
J. Sainsbury: 44
Suffolk County Council: back
    cover(top), 8, 8-9, 10(bottom), 11,
    21(top)
Surrey County Council: 6
John Topham Picture Library: 4, 14, 31,
    32(bottom), 33, 37(top), 38, 40,
    40-41, 41, 42(top and bottom), 43
Welsh Folk Museum: 28

Picture research by Caroline Mitchell

Contents

Introduction

In 1859, when this book starts, railways were quite new, cars had not been invented, and flying was just a fantasy. Now, of course, men have been to the moon and 'walked' in space.

Shops and shopping have changed, too. The shopkeepers shown here, and their customers, would scarcely recognize today's high streets. Most were used to small family shops and bustling markets selling only local goods and seasonal foods. The book traces how these gradually became the big chain stores we know, with an enormous range of goods on sale.

Although improved transport helped to bring this about, people's attitudes to shopping have also changed. When Gordon Selfridge (see page 24) visited Britain in the 1890s he was amazed to find that everyone – shoppers and shopkeepers – believed that shops were there only to supply what a customer asked for. In fact, in many of the smartest shops, the customers sat at a counter and the goods they wanted were brought to them. They had no opportunity to look around at other things to buy. This was no longer the case in America, where manufacturers, advertisers and shopkeepers all worked together to create a demand for their goods.

Gordon Selfridge set out to introduce American ideas to the British shopper. He used advertising to publicise his store and its goods. You only have to look at all today's advertisements to know his ideas were successful.

Advertising plays a crucial part in modern shopping. Manufacturers spend vast sums telling us about their products. The children below, photographed in 1953, are celebrating the end of sweet rationing, part of the strict control of food supplies during the Second World War. For the first time they can buy whatever sweets they like: but advertising helps them, and you, to choose from the great range now available.

A long queue outside a sweetshop, on the day sweet rationing ended, 1953.

HOW TO USE THIS BOOK

The photos in this book give a good idea of the changes in the lives of shoppers and shopkeepers over the last century and a quarter, and also of how little some things have changed.

As you read through the book, look out for the things that are different from today, and also for the things that are the same. You can tell, too, from people's expressions what they are thinking, and that certainly hasn't changed!

Learn to look closely at the photographs and to draw conclusions from what you see. Although they were never intended as such, all the photographs in this book are important documents in our social history.

The date at the top of each page tells you when the photograph was taken.

A NOTE ABOUT PHOTOGRAPHY

In the 1850s, when this book starts, photography was very much a new and unusual hobby, a pastime for a few scientifically-minded amateurs with servants to carry the heavy, cumbersome equipment. Taking photographs was a laborious process. The sitter had to stay absolutely still for several minutes while the image developed on the photographic plate. Any movement, however slight, would come out as a blur.

Early photographs were processed onto metal and glass as well as paper. Improvements came first through the experiments of individuals, usually working alone to solve problems. Early great pioneers included Henry Fox Talbot, Frederick Scott Archer and the Frenchman, Louis Daguerre. Their discoveries made photography what it is today.

With today's cameras it is possible for anyone to take a photo – just point the lens and snap! But that hasn't reduced photography's important role as a recorder of history – the history of individuals as well as great events. Every photograph, however ordinary, can be considered an historical document. As you will discover in this book, there's a lot you can learn from a photograph!

The photograph below was taken in 1907. Cameras were already much simpler than in the very early days of photography, but were still slow and difficult to use.

GUILDFORD HIGH STREET

Guildford High Street (left), photographed here in 1859, was typical of high streets in prosperous market towns throughout Britain. Although smooth macadamed roads had been introduced in the 1820s, cobblestones were still used to help horses get a grip on wet, slippery or steep streets.

Notice the fine Georgian architecture of the two buildings in which Gill & Carling and Frank Lasham have their shops. The curtains in the upstairs windows suggest that these two shopkeepers lived above their businesses – a very usual custom.

The shop of 'Wood, Tailor and Clothier' is different. The original building looks as if it has been modernized, and new windows have been put in on the first floor. This floor is obviously used as part of the business (you can see dummies in the two middle windows) and not as the Woods' family home. Perhaps Mr Wood, and his partners White and Tucker, were more enterprising businessmen than some of their high street colleagues.

(And if anyone tries to tell you that venetian blinds are new, then show them the windows above Wood's and Lasham's shops and remind them of the date of this photograph!)

You may think the high street looks very deserted. Certainly there are not many shoppers in the photograph. But this reflects the state of photography, not the shops. Photographic images were still registered on specially treated glass plates (film had not been invented). This needed long exposures to capture the scene being photographed. If something moved during the exposure it usually looked blurred in the photograph, like the boys on the left. So the photographer probably waited till there were few people about, or else asked them not to walk down the street until he had taken his photo, which could be for several minutes.

A BANK

This bank interior was photographed in Taunton, Somerset, in 1866. And what a splendid interior it is: the walls panelled and decorated and the counter with its wooden panels, marble top and imposing lights.

The polished brass scales on the counter were for weighing coins, to check how much money customers brought in. Until the First World War (1914-18) the lowest value note was £5. This was a great deal of money, and most people used only coins for their shopping and everyday needs. Notes were quite rare. Modern banks still use scales, though rather different from the ones shown here. See if you can spot them next time you visit a bank.

Today most banks belong to 'the big four', but they have branches all over the country. In Victorian times it was quite different: there were hundreds of banks, each operating in a particular part of the country. The bank in this photograph is the Taunton branch of the West of England and South Wales District Bank. Gradually the more successful banks expanded taking over less successful ones and spreading throughout the country.

There were no government controls over banks in those days. They were just like any business and, like all businesses, could go bankrupt. When this happened everyone with money in the bank lost it. This is why many people distrusted banks. Fortunately the same cannot happen today because of the strict laws that regulate banking.

Have you noticed the complete lack of security measures in the bank? Even the wrought-iron grilles at the back look more for privacy and decoration than for protection. Clearly they did not expect to be raided.

A SHOE SHOP

The two photographs on this page were taken in Ipswich, Suffolk, in the 1870s. Crowded shop windows were obviously the fashion then, though in this shoe shop (left) artificial plants and fruit have at least been used in an attempt at display. (If you wonder why the photograph looks a bit odd at the top, it is because the glass window is reflecting the building opposite.)

What an array of boots and shoes! But notice how dark most of the shoes are. The great variety of colours we are used to is something quite new. There are no shoes in synthetic materials either. Every-

THE DRAPER'S SHOP

What a contrast the crowded windows of A. G. Cross make to those we are used to now. And to be doubly certain that people could see their goods, they even installed their own shopfront lighting. Notice how the glass panels of the lanterns that are facing the street are opaque, while those facing the shop window are transparent, to throw as much light as possible on the goods for sale.

Read the notices on the windows and try to pick out the items advertised. There are many plain straw hats. If you bought one, you could have it trimmed for free. The next year, if you wanted a change, they would put on new trimmings for only a small charge. There is also a good selection of 'Sailor hats with broad brims specially suitable for young ladies' in the second window.

The 'New blouses and shirts' are displayed each side of the doorway. The blouses all have nipped-in waists and sleeves puffed up on the shoulder.

'The value and variety in CAPES of every class, cloth, velvet etc' which they proudly advertise are in the farthest window. Capes were the most practical garments for women to wear over their long, full skirts, although the enormous crinolines of the 1840s and 1850s were no longer fashionable.

The four white bonnets in the nearest window are 'Sunday best' versions of the bonnets country women wore when working in the fields. Made of thick creamy-white cotton, and beautifully shaped with tucks, the frills were more than just decoration – they protected the wearer's face and neck from the sun when she was helping with the harvest.

thing was made of leather, although party shoes, like those under the glass domes to keep them clean, might be of satin.

All the boots in this window are for women, mainly neat ankle boots for everyday wear. With all that lacing there was no chance of kicking them off to let your feet have a rest on a busy day. But many of these styles were no more 'sensible' than today's. Small feet were fashionable so people crammed their feet into shoes as small as possible. And if that led to corns, bunions and distorted toes, it was considered a small price to pay for fashion.

1875

SECONDHAND FURNITURE

Not everyone could afford the new furniture and toys shown in the photograph below. Britain was one of the wealthiest countries in the world in the last part of the nineteenth century, but there was also a great deal of poverty. It was probably worst in the industrial towns and cities; in the country most people had some land where they could grow vegetables or keep a few chickens.

The photograph on the right was taken in London, but it could just as well have been in Birmingham, Manchester or Liverpool. On the pavement outside a tiny shop in the poor part of town, the secondhand furniture dealer piles up his goods. There's no attempt at display. Chairs balance awkwardly on top of each other. The cane-seated one (you can see the shadow of the seat's pattern on the edge of the pavement) probably started life in the nursery of a middle-class home. Smart coats and capes once hung from the coatrack on the chair's seat, and a pet canary sang in the battered little cage under the table. Now they will be sold for a few pence.

A CHRISTMAS DISPLAY

Christmas was as popular with shop-keepers 100 years ago as it is today. With customers willing to spend more than at any other time of the year, rival shops vied with each other in the lavishness of their displays.

From a series of old photographs we know that this butcher in Ipswich, Suffolk (right), made a special feature of displays like this each Christmas. It is certainly eyecatching. From the branch of mistletoe at the top to the piglets on the table in front of the window there is no doubt what he has in stock.

Can you identify the various meats? There are sides of beef and mutton, as well as pork, turkeys and rabbits. And can you spot the pheasants? The string of sausages is homemade. Butchers prided them-selves on their sausage recipes.

For the rest of the year, roast joints were a popular favourite in late Victorian times – families were large and joints were a practical way of feeding them if you could afford it. For families like the furniture dealer and his wife opposite, however, it was much more likely to be a few chops on good days and 'a pen'orth of lights' on bad ones. That's about a ½p's worth of the lungs from sheep or pigs.

TOYS AND FANCY GOODS

(Left) The outside of his shop cer-tainly justifies J. Redstone of Ipswich's claim to have the 'Largest choice, best assortment of toys, fan-cy goods, dolls'. Look at the range: trains, rocking horse, hoops, cra-dles, dolls' prams, bats. There are also plenty of baskets on sale.

But Mr Redstone, standing at his shop door, stocked other things, too. The mangle, in the other doorway, looks strongly made and is on wheels, making it easy to move into position for wringing out the clothes on washday. He's enterprising too, offering an early form of hire pur-chase on many of his goods.

DEVONPORT

Devonport, with its associations with Plymouth and the Royal Navy, was a thriving place at the end of the last century. This busy scene is typical of similar towns up and down the country at this time.

Britain's extensive Empire provided cheap raw materials for industry, and a ready market for manufactured goods. This brought great wealth to the country. However, there were already warning signs that this could not last. The Empire market was virtually a captive one – British manufacturers faced little

competition there – and Germany and America were rapidly catching up on Britain's industrial lead.

But, for the people photographed here, out and about in the sunshine, such matters were not their concern. They could enjoy the town's broad pavements and clean streets. There were plenty of cabs (horse-drawn) for hire, but not so much traffic that the streets became jammed. (The authorities in London at this time were worried because there was so much horse-drawn traffic in the West End that there were constant traffic

jams, and the horse droppings were thought to be a health hazard.)

This photo is also interesting because it shows the great improvements that had taken place in photography. Although this is a busy street and people are obviously moving about, there is little blurring in the picture. Look at some of the earlier photographs and see how everyone is standing very still or, if they move, they are blurred. It is not surprising that people in early photos sometimes look rather grim – they had to remain still for several minutes.

PETTICOAT LANE, LONDON

This is London's famous Petticoat Lane street market in 1895. What a contrast it is to the wide, prosperous middle-class shopping streets of Devonport opposite.

This market is in a narrow street of grimy buildings in one of the poorest parts of the city. Compare the people's clothes. There are no smartly dressed men in this street, only a few bowlers among the cloth caps. There are no carriages either, just heavy pushbarrows. Everyone and everything looks a bit shabby, an impression accentuated by the broken street lamp and shored-up buildings on the left. Can you see the policeman on patrol, with a row of shiny buttons down his tunic? Even though this was a poor area, pickpockets were still common.

Have you noticed how many people are looking towards the camera? Photography was still rather a novelty, and from the angle of this picture the photographer was obviously quite high up – about level with the top of the lamp-post. Perhaps he was leaning out of a window or balancing on top of a ladder. However he took his picture, it clearly made an entertaining change from the usual market gossip.

You could buy most things in Petticoat Lane – and you still can, for the market continues to thrive. In many ways it hasn't changed much. Fish may not come out of a barrel any more (far right), and it may be easier to buy green peppers and avocadoes than swedes and parsnips, but there are still rails of cheap clothes and stallholders shouting their wares. But now no-one takes any notice of tourists taking photos.

13

MARKET DAY

Market day was the week's high-spot in country towns, though the pouring rain probably made this one at Llanrwst in North Wales in 1896 rather dreary. People came from the surrounding farms and villages to buy and sell. Farmers drove their cattle to market on foot – there were no lorries or trucks, and all transport was horse-drawn. See how the cattle are steaming in the damp air.

While the farmer sold his cattle and bought grain and seed, his wife usually went shopping. Perhaps she needed a broom like the ones hanging outside 'H. Ffraid Williams, House Furnisher'. Or maybe it was time for a new corset. The two white shapes in the window of the Misses Roberts' 'Bon Marché' are corsets. All women wore these hot heavy undergarments. They were usually made of cotton and webbing, with whalebone to stiffen and shape them.

Although ready-made clothes were by now quite common, many women still made their families' clothes. The material would come from drapers like the Bon Marché. There were only natural fibres such as wool, linen and cotton; light, easy-care man-made fibres are very recent inventions. Notice, too, how

A MARKET HALL

Market halls, like the one below in Burnley, became quite a feature of Victorian towns, especially in the new industrial centres where there was either no tradition of a weekly market or the town's rapid growth made it quite inadequate.

The market halls were popular because they were convenient – they were covered, protected from the elements, and they functioned every day. Look how gaily the hall is decorated with flags and the way everyone is looking at the camera. This is obviously a special occasion, though sadly we have no information about what they are celebrating.

The two women in the foreground may be stallholders who brought their china to the market hall in the big wicker basket behind them. If you look carefully you can see the woman on the left is wearing a cotton bonnet – the dark stripe at the top of her head is a fold in the bonnet. Bonnets were unusual in an industrial town like Burnley; all the other women in the photograph are wearing boaters or wide brimmed hats.

The 'Incandescent GAS GLOBES' that John Harrison is advertising are fancy light fittings to go over the jet of flame on a gas light. From the display in his window, he obviously also sells the large ornate vases that graced most Victorian mantlepieces. You can see them sometimes now in antique or junk shops.

dark all the clothes are. It is not just because the day is wet and everyone is wearing dark overcoats and shawls. The bright colours we are used to were not available – there were no dyes from chemicals.

If it had been a good day and the cattle had fetched a good price, the children might get some Fry's chocolate, advertised for sale on the window of 'M. Williams, Confectioner'.

LEICESTER MARKET

Two views of Leicester market: the top one was taken in the summer – look at the long skirts and blouses and the hats – and the other when it was cold enough for shawls and capes, and the stalls did not need awnings to keep off the sun. If you look for the statue in both pictures you can tell whereabouts in the market the bottom photo was taken.

Apart from the seasons, there is little change between the two photos. Turner & Co have their shops at 34, 36 and 38 (look at the fire escape stairs on the roof). G. H. Durrant's baby linen warehouse is at Regent House. (Shopkeepers used the term 'warehouse' when they wanted to show their business was bigger than just a shop.) There is the 6½d Bazaar at the Silver Arcade, and Sturges's Drug Stores next door.

But in the background of the picture at the top are signs of change – the tall chimneys of the industrial areas that were beginning to surround this old market square.

Here as elsewhere industrialization led to the loss of many regional characteristics – including English cheeses. It is many, many years since Leicester cheese was sold like this in the market square. And modern health regulations would make it quite impossible for cheese to be displayed for sale on straw-covered cobblestones!

THE SADDLER'S SHOP

By the early twentieth century, the days of the horse as the chief form of transport were almost over. For a short time yet, however, there would still be shops like this one at Camberley in Surrey in every town and large village in the country.

Can you identify any of the harness? The odd-looking 'saddles' each side of the shop doorway are for horses pulling carts or carriages. The reins went through the pair of metal rings at the top, and the shafts went through the leather loops each side. The thick leather strap hanging down was unbuckled to go round the horse's girth and hold everything in place.

Look at the notice on the delivery trap. Portmanteaus are trunks. There is one on the back – no need for lightweight aircraft luggage then!

A PAWNBROKER

Pawnbrokers provided an essential service in a poor community, lending money without charging interest. Instead the borrower left something with the pawnbroker. It did not really matter what it was as long as it was good enough to sell. If the borrower did not repay (or 'redeem') the debt in time, the pawnbroker put the pawned item up for sale.

Whysall's shop in Leicester, with the pawnbroker's traditional sign of three hanging balls (top right), tells a sad story of poverty and debt. Counterpanes and hearth rugs are not absolutely essential in a home, and perhaps the girls had outgrown their little dresses. But what did a man wear if his boots were on sale in the pawnshop? If he'd had to borrow money, he probably did not even have a second pair.

Rentday was always busy for the pawnbroker, as people borrowed money to pay the rent. Fridays were also often busy. Many people would redeem their Sunday best clothes on a Friday, and return them to the pawnshop on Monday morning.

FURNITURE SHOWROOM

Anyone shopping for new furniture in Leicester in 1900 would have plenty to choose from here! But what a jumble it is, with no attractive displays to make customers want to buy. All the different styles have just been dumped down together.

Notice the dark wood used for the furniture, quite a contrast to today. Imagine how dark homes must have been at this time. As well as dark furniture, it was fashionable to have dark curtains, dark carpets *and* dark wallpaper.

Most of this furniture can now only be found in antique or junk shops. However, the high-backed 'Queen Anne' sofa and two chairs on the right are still a popular style, and you can see them today – some 270 years after the death of the Queen from whom they get their name.

18

A LONDON DRESSMAKER

(Right) Only the very rich could afford clothes like this. The long velvet train suggests that this is a dress for a specially grand occasion – at court, perhaps.

Look at the colour and length of the dress. Since floors get dirty, even in palaces and grand houses, you can imagine what colour the hem would be after a night out. In fact the hems of most dresses had ribbons, fringes or binding sewn on to stop the actual dress material from getting dirty as it rubbed along floors and pavements. The edging could be changed whenever necessary without spoiling the dress.

Notice the woman's reflection in the mirror. In keeping with the fashion of the time her chest and bottom stick out, giving her a hollow back which was very uncomfortable. Women did not have to remember to hold themselves like this – their corsets did it for them.

The dressmaker's room is very grand, with its high ceiling and elaborate decoration. But the seamstress kneeling on the floor to alter the train almost certainly made this dress somewhere else, probably in a small cramped workroom, working long hours for very little money.

19

NEWSAGENT

Apart from the lettering used for the sign, this could be a newsagent in a back street today. Even the newspaper headlines seem strangely familiar.

Advertised on the window are the children's comics *Chums* and *Little Folks*. For the rest of the family there are *The Penny Magazine, Cassell's Saturday Journal, The Home Milliner*

and *Building World*.

And what an enormous variety of postcards: pin-ups, both male and female, scenic views and cuddly animals, and cards with your sweetheart's name on, Sybil, Marie, Dick or Ruth. Postcards were used much more often to send messages years ago, when there were few telephones, and postal rates were cheap.

GREENGROCER

The bundles of holly, Christmas trees and mistletoe for sale must mean this photo (right) was taken around Christmas time. The custom for Christmas trees had been introduced to Britain by Prince Albert, Queen Victoria's husband, and so was relatively new when this 'noted shop for potatoes' was photographed. But it was obviously a popular custom if a small greengrocer in Suffolk was selling the trees.

The shop itself does not look so very different from some country shops today. There are no peppers or aubergines, but the cabbages are handsome and there are bananas, though it is rare now to see a hand of them – one is propped up by the wheel of the pushcart. Improved transport enabled such luxuries to be brought from overseas.

Look at the large bunches of celery. It may be much cheaper than what we get today, but cleaning it was a chore. The rabbits hanging above the window were obviously a profitable sideline.

The onions on the right were strung up to make them easier to store, while the barrels in the centre contained locally-grown potatoes, this shop's speciality.

PETFOOD SELLER

(Left) This man was sure of a warm welcome wherever he went. There was no KiteKat, Chappie or Pedigree Chum for these cats and dogs. Instead, men like Frank Butcher (do you think that was his real name?) pushed their barrows round the streets selling horse meat as pet food. Horses were still the most usual form of transport, so there was always a good supply of old carcases to provide cheap meat.

Behind old Mr Butcher stands a boy with a milk pail. He's been to the dairy to get some fresh milk. Other families might use tinned milk such as Viking or Nestlés, as advertised on the wall in the background.

21

SWAN & EDGAR

The early years of this century, before the outbreak of the First World War (1914), were the great days of the department store. We take them for granted now, but when Kendal Milne & Faulkener of Manchester first opened in 1836 their idea of the same shop selling completely different goods in separate departments was revolutionary. Most of the stores started as drapers, selling household linens, dress materials and trimmings, although Harrods started as a grocers.

William Edgar and John Swan, the two men who founded Swan & Edgar

in Piccadilly, London, in 1812, had very humble beginnings. They were stallholders, probably in nearby St James's Market which was 'avoided by all persons who respected their characters or their garments' – a great contrast to the eminently respectable store photographed here nearly 100 years later.

Notice the three royal coats of arms over the entrance, showing that it supplied goods to members of the royal family.

(If you ever read Somerset Maugham's book *Of Human Bondage*, the descriptions of Lynn & Sed-

ley, the store where the hero, Philip Carey, works, are really based on Swan & Edgar.)

Although there are still horses and carts, motor cars and motor buses are beginning to appear. And telephone wires are beginning to sprout from the rooftops. The road, however, is still cobbled. The two street lamps are gas lights; each evening a lamp-lighter came round to turn them on.

HUNTING FOR BARGAINS

Fashionable bargain hunters throng the pavement outside Barkers of Kensington, London, during the last few days of the summer sales.

Look at the hats! The size of them! And these were ordinary, everyday, 'going shopping' hats, not grand occasion ones. They take up enough room on a crowded pavement, but they must have seemed even larger in their hatboxes at home. Fortu-

nately the homes of prosperous people like these were spacious.

In contrast to the hats, see how small the handbags are. These women carried no credit or bank cards, few would have had cheque books or car keys, and 'respectable' women did not wear make-up. They probably did not carry much money either, because all the big stores and many smaller shops were happy to

have account customers. Once a month they would receive a bill for everything they had bought.

Most shops had their own delivery service. That is why not one of these shoppers is burdened with bulging carrier bags. Vans took the big items and errand boys, like the one here with the pile of parcels, delivered the small things. So shopping really could be a pleasure! 23

1908

LADIES' UNDERWEAR

The advertisement below appeared in *The Queen, the Lady's Magazine.* The nightdresses (top) and bedjackets (bottom) may look rather fussy to us, but they were really quite daring in their day.

Throughout Victoria's reign (1837-1901) pretty underclothes were frowned on. They were not 'nice', and no respectable woman wore them. Gradually, however, attitudes changed. This was helped by 'Lucile', who ran one of the most successful, and expensive, dressmaking businesses in London. When she first introduced pretty and rather flimsy underclothes in the 1890s, her customers 'slowly one by one slunk into the shop in a rather shamefaced way and departed carrying an inconspicuous parcel'. Although 'one or two returned to bring the new purchases sorrowfully back because a husband had put his foot down' the majority came back to order more.

Now, in chain stores in every high street in the country hang underclothes that would have given a respectable Victorian a heart-attack or hysterics.

LADIES' OUTFITTERS

The rich and the fashionable are a minority in any society. Though the department stores drew thousands of customers, most women still bought their clothes at shops like the one in the photograph above at Egham in Surrey.

Such shops were smaller and much less fashionable, but they were friendly. The big city department stores, with their dignified assistants in tail coats, were a far cry from these two smiling women and their dog. The window of their shop is as crowded as earlier ones in this book, though even department stores then crammed their windows.

Change, however, was in the air. In 1909, the American, Gordon Selfridge, opened his store in London's Oxford Street. He introduced many new ideas to Britain. One was a completely different style of window display. Instead of windows crammed with cheap goods, shoppers in Oxford Street were treated to dramatic displays of fewer but higher quality goods. And the displays were lit until midnight to attract people out for the evening. We know his methods were successful because the other stores soon copied them.

But it would be a long time before such ideas reached shops like this one, with its friendly clutter of collars, gloves, linen, wools and 'Serpenta corsets'. In fact, away from the main shopping streets, you can still find shops today whose windows look much more like this than anything Gordon Selfridge brought with him from America.

A HATSHOP

This hat shop in Dorchester, Dorset, has put on a wonderful display of spring and summer hats to attract customers.

The flowers in the window are not just window dressing. They are on sale too, for trimming hats. Everyone in those days wore hats, men as well as women. But hats do not wear out like shoes, or get lost like gloves. So a new hat was often considered an unnecessary extravagance, while changing the look of an old one by retrimming it was not. Ribbons, lace and artificial flowers were the most usual trimmings. Sadly, however, the feathers of exotic birds were also very fashionable.

This is a country milliner and, as you can see, the styles are not extreme. It's also possible to see some of the prices. Except for the most fancy hats, prices here are very similar to those in A.G. Cross's window (page 8). That photograph was taken 40 years earlier than this one – which just goes to show how little inflation there was at this time.   25

A GROCER

The sign above Hunters of Clwyd proudly proclaims they are 'Expert tea blenders'. Expert or not, many grocers made up their own blends of tea. The brands we are familiar with did not dominate the shelves.

Although the windows are full of tins and jars, Hunters' customers did not have a wide choice of ready-packed goods. Most items like pulses, dried fruit, sugar, flour and rice were stored in large bins. Each customer's order was scooped into a thick paper bag. Butter was kept on marble slabs on the counter. It was measured out and patted into a block, and then wrapped. Bacon, perhaps 'farm fed' like that hanging outside the shop, was cut to order, too.

Hunters are also 'Provision importers', but they could only import things that travelled well – dried or tinned goods, mostly. Until the coming of refrigeration, many of the perishable things we take for granted, foreign cheeses for exam-ple, could not survive a long journey.

Have a look at some of the other things Hunters stock: hearth rugs, wicker chairs, occasional tables, coal boxes, frying pans and washing dollies. The dollies are the long wooden things with a six-legged stool at the end. On washday you paddled a dolly around among the clothes and sheets in the washtub to help get the dirt out.

And have you noticed (left) that special offers with money-off coupons are nothing new?

SELLING MILK

Scenes like this one above at Builth
Wells in Powys were common in
country towns and villages. The
milkman, with a shiny milkchurn on
his cart, went from door to door,
measuring milk from the churn into
his customers' own containers. You
can see here that he is holding two
small measures.

Beyond the cart is a sign, 'Com-
mercial and Family Boarding House,
Temperance Hotel'. The word
'temperance' means that the hotel
did not serve alcohol.

A TRIPE DRESSER

(Right) Tripe was a popular food for
poor people in Victorian and Edwardian times. It was prepared from the
stomachs of sheep and cows by spe-
cialist tripe dressers like Alfred
Cooper of Burnley, Lancashire, and
was a cheap way to feed the family.
Tripe and onions was a particular
speciality of the Midlands and North
of England, probably because the
great industrial cities were there –
and the poverty that went with them.
Mr Cooper clearly had links with the
local slaughterhouse, because tallow
(left-hand window) is made from
animal carcases too.

Mr Cooper was obviously an enterprising businessman – his shop is
on the 'phone. Many of the London
stores had 'phones by this time, but
not many small businesses in the provinces.

THE CHEMIST

John Bees stands in his chemist's shop in Llantwit Major, Glamorgan, almost glaring at the camera. Shelf upon shelf of glass jars, each one labelled in Latin, contain his stock – the powders from which he makes up remedies for his customers' various illnesses.

Before the introduction of the National Health Service in 1948, doctors used to charge for seeing patients, so many poor people relied on the chemist for advice. If you had to see the doctor and could not pay all his fee at once, you could often pay it by instalments – a few pence each week until the debt was paid off.

John Bees' shelves also show how few ready-made medicines there were. Beecham's Pills, introduced in 1842, were one of the first and most successful. (Their powders did not appear on the market until 1926.) To help their customers, many chemists mixed their own patent cures for common ailments.

Have a look at Mr Bees' other shelves. The bottles on them look very like bottles of wine or spirits, and he also has two Sparklet soda water syphons in stock. Perhaps some of his customers believed that alcohol had medicinal properties!

Incidentally, the mark running from top to bottom of the picture is a flaw in the negative from which the original photograph was made.

ELECTRICITY

Electric lighting was as varied as now when this showroom in Northampton was photographed in 1924. Many of the light fittings on display here can still be found in homes up and down the country.

Spot some of the styles: the swirls of 'Art Nouveau', the swags and ribbons of imitation 'Georgian', and the Victorian love of fringing. Many of the lampshades are so heavy that they look as if they would cut out most of the light. See, too, the 'classical' figures with light fittings sprouting from their heads on the righthand windowsill – then, the latest word in elegance.

The electric fires look much too small to heat a room. They also look unsafe. They would be very easy to knock over and a small child could put its fingers through the protective wires and get badly burnt. But being able to turn them on and off at the flick of a switch was luxury compared to the old coal fires.

A CLEVER SLOGAN?

Photographed in Oxford in 1929, the sign says everything (although modern advertising agencies would probably think it wrong to use 'NOT' so early in a slogan).

Remember the ads on A.G. Cross's shop (page 8).

ADVERTISING

This wall of advertisements (right) was photographed in Leicester in 1935. The Universal Billposting Company rented the wall from the owners, and has obviously tried to cram in as many advertisements as possible – there is scarcely a spare square inch of space!

The small posters are low down so they can be read by passers-by. The bigger ones are placed higher, to catch the eye. And any gaps are put to good use advertising the posters themselves.

The advertising industry today is vast and important. Manufacturers spend millions of pounds each year telling us about their products. The growth of the advertising industry has happened in the last 30 years, but advertisements are nothing new. Remember the ads on A.G. Cross's shop (page 8).

Not all the products advertised here are still available. But although 50 years old, the posters themselves look quite familiar. That's because many advertisers today use an old-fashioned design and illustration to give their product a traditional feel.

THE HABERDASHER

What a jumble there is in this haberdasher's shop in Kensington, London. Here are no neat racks of colour-graded zips or cotton reels from which to help yourself, no stands of ready-packed pins, needles or buttons, just a clutter which looks as if it has been there for ages and where you might find almost anything.

No wonder there were chairs for customers to sit on while the shopkeeper searched for what was wanted. But at least shoppers could buy exactly the number of buttons they needed – and not end up with too many because the buttons are all pre-packed.

Look at the vast range of goods in the shop: tape measures, dressing gown cords, string, coat hangers, hair bows, dyes...

The Bear Brand advertisements are for stockings, not tights (these have become popular only in the last 20 years or so). Before, women wore stockings and kept them up with suspender belts or the suspenders on their corsets.

Most stockings, for everyday wear, came in thick beige crêpe, with a seam down the back of the leg. Because they did not stretch much, stockings were made in the shape of the leg and foot, and you bought them according to the size of your feet, not your hips.

The amount of string for sale is revealing, too. There were no staples then, nor sticky tape like Sellotape. All parcels were done up with string, and sometimes sealing wax was used as well.

THE PEDLAR

Pedlars, like the one here in Worcestershire (left), travelled round the countryside in all weathers carrying their goods in a pack – just as they had done for centuries. They sold many small items: pins, needles, sewing cottons, darning wools, buttons and hair clips.

Notice the strong leather carrying strap on this pedlar's pack, and the thinner one to keep the lid open. When business is finished he rolls up the braces slung over his shoulder, puts them in the box, flaps the side leaves (you can see the one with the hair grips on it) across the top, lets the top down and folds the front flap across everything. Then he's off to the next lonely cottage.

Before people had cars, pedlars provided an essential service in remote areas.

A TRAVELLING SHOP

Travelling shops (right) were another way of reaching customers. This converted van has special display windows, and a bell on the bonnet to let people know their shop has arrived. Some of the items on sale are still available now.

Many customers bought goods 'on account' and paid for everything at the end of each month. This meant that shopkeepers had to wait for their money. To encourage people to pay for goods when they bought them, shopkeepers often offered a discount – a slightly lower price. That's what the sign 'Cash Prices' on the van door means.

A TRAVELLING SALESMAN

This salesman travelled round the small villages and lonely farms of Devon in the 1930s. Cars were luxuries and buses slow, so people relied on travelling salesmen for everyday household goods.

The things on this crowded cart show us what people used in their homes. Notice how almost everything is made of metal or wood – today's plastics and polythene had not yet been invented.

Many homes, especially in the country, had no running water. All the water needed for cooking, washing and drinking had to be carried in buckets from a well. The buckets like those on the cart, and outside the cottage opposite, were made of heavy grey galvanised or white enamelled metal.

On the back of the cart hang two washboards – rectangular wooden frames with a ridged sheet of wood across the frame. Clothes were rubbed up and down the ridged surface to get the dirt out.

Above the washboards is a light, rather bent-looking square. This is a meat-safe. Fridges were even rarer than cars. Instead, most homes had a larder – a special large cupboard or small room – in which food was kept. Larders were usually on the north, the coolest, side of the house, and the food was stored in large tins or earthenware crocks. Food not kept in these was covered with a 'safe', a gauze-covered frame to keep flies off. Now that most food comes prepacked, flies are no longer such a problem.

The three photographs shown here were all taken on the same day in the market place at Gainsborough in Lincolnshire.

For one day a week market squares in country towns throughout the British Isles became bustling shopping centres for the surrounding villages. The stallholders, too, had a regular weekly round of markets. One day each week they might be in Gainsborough, as here, the next in another Lincolnshire town such as Boston, then perhaps to Spalding and so on, regularly round the year.

SHOE STALL

Look at the boots and shoes on the stall above. Heavy leather boots like these were common in country areas where most men worked on farms. They needed something tough for many of them still walked miles across fields each year behind horse-drawn farm implements. There were no synthetic soles in those days, and almost all shoes were made of real leather throughout, including the lining and sole.

'The Gamekeeper', the brand name on the box, tells its own story. Every country estate and many large farms had at least one gamekeeper to keep down vermin like rats, rabbits and foxes. His was a year-round out-of-doors job, and so a good advertisement for strong boots. Today, shoe stalls in country markets are more likely to be selling Wellington boots and trainers.

VEGETABLE STALL

(Left) The spring onions, radishes and lettuces on sale here were probably grown locally, in allotments and smallholdings.

The big market gardeners usually sold all their produce to a wholesaler, based at one of the few huge central markets (Covent Garden in London was the most famous). The wholesaler in turn supplied greengrocers and fruiterers all round the country.

A country market, however, was an ideal place for a small local grower to sell his produce. A market pitch and trestle table are cheap to rent. And in turn the customer knows that 'freshly picked' means just that.

SELLING LINO

Photographs can often tell you much more than at first seems obvious. Above, for example, is a man selling linoleum (lino for short), calling out to attract passers-by.

From this you can move to the less obvious: what people had on the floors of their homes. Lino was then the best thing available. Easy-care vinyls and fitted carpets were still in the future, and for these shoppers lino was a great improvement on wooden boards, quarry tiles or floor bricks, all of which needed regular and strenuous scrubbing.

Look at the patterns on the lino and compare them with modern flooring. And have a look, too, at the salesmen and their customers. When were you last served by someone wearing a waistcoat, stiff butterfly collar and bow tie? Notice, too, how all the shoppers are wearing hats. 35

FROME MARKET

This photo was taken in Frome in Somerset, a small and busy market town. Although some of the produce here probably came from local growers, some also came from a wholesaler – as you can see from the boxes stacked on the left.

Have you noticed what people are carrying their shopping in? Stout shopping baskets and, here, a paper carrier bag. The light, colourful carriers and PVC shopping bags we are used to are very new. Shopping baskets may last longer, but they also weigh a great deal more, even when empty.

Next time you pass a Boots, have a look at the sign and compare it with the one in this picture. What are the most obvious differences – or aren't there any?

A MARKET IN IRELAND

What a contrast this calm market in Mitchelstown in Eire (right) makes to the bustling street in the photograph above it.

However, the goods on sale here are the same as in any market – clothes, food, rugs, pictures, china. Can you spot the big wooden crates the stallholders pack their wares in?

Look at the baskets in the lefthand corner of the photo. Have they been brought to market on the pony cart nearby? On the back of the cart is a pile of what look like the spars used to make baskets.

Interestingly, there are more bare heads in this picture than in any others so far. Maybe it's summer. The trees and piled hay cart suggest this, even though the old ladies are well wrapped up in their shawls.

DARTFORD MARKET

Shops and stalls compete for custom in this street (left), photographed in Dartford, Kent, in 1936.

Some of the shop signs show clearly in the photograph, with names of shops that we use today – Burton, Boots, Dolcis. But others, like 'Mence Smith Household Stores' have disappeared, probably taken over by larger, more successful companies.

The Boots here and in Frome (opposite) illustrate a growing shopping trend which gathered pace after the First World War, and still continues: the growth of chain stores. For centuries most town and village shops were owned and run by the shopkeeper and perhaps his family. If he was successful he might open another shop in a neighbouring town and employ someone to run it for him. But unless he was very successful, he seldom had enough money to open many more.

Shops belonging to a chain, however, are run by managers, not owners. The shops actually belong to a company which usually operates from an office block, not a shop. Sometimes the company owning the chain makes the goods the shops sell. Boots, based in Nottingham, started as a chemist shop, is a large manufacturer of drugs, and now sells many other things

SALES SPREE

You see photographs of scenes like this in the papers and on television every time, winter and summer, that the big department stores hold their sales.

But there's one big difference between this picture, taken in Barkers of Kensington, London, and what you're likely to see today – the customers now will not be fighting over hats. Hats are no longer an important part of a woman's clothes. They are still worn, of course, but usually only in cold weather or for special occasions.

One of the assistants in the background looks very pleased at what is going on. The 'Special Offer' and the 3/11 hats 'As advertised' are popular with the customers. Because money values have changed so much it is hard to say what these hats would be sold for now – that is, if anyone would buy them!

Notice what the shoppers are wearing and compare it with some of the earlier photographs in this book. Skirts are shorter and hats smaller, but look how much bigger the handbags are compared with the tiny ones carried by the Kensington shoppers of 30 years earlier (on page 23).

ELECTRIC APPLIANCES

(Right) These, believe it or not, were quite the latest in electric appliances in 1938. And in the background stands a cardboard cut-out of the advertiser's idea of the delighted housewife who uses them.

This display, in an electricity showroom, shows the development of a simpler, less cluttered way of attracting customers – in keeping with electricity's clean and modern image.

If the appliances seem laughably old-fashioned, remember they really were an enormous improvement on what many housewives were used to. These cookers worked the moment they were turned on, the temperature of oven and hot-plates could be changed by turning a switch, they were small and light-coloured.

Before, it was much more common to have a combined cooker and boiler fired by coal. This meant it had to be filled up several times a day. Besides being heavy to carry, coal is also dirty and makes a lot of ash.

To cook, you had to wait for the fire to heat the oven or hot-plates, which could take time. Only experience taught when the oven reached the right temperature because there was no thermostat or warning light, and

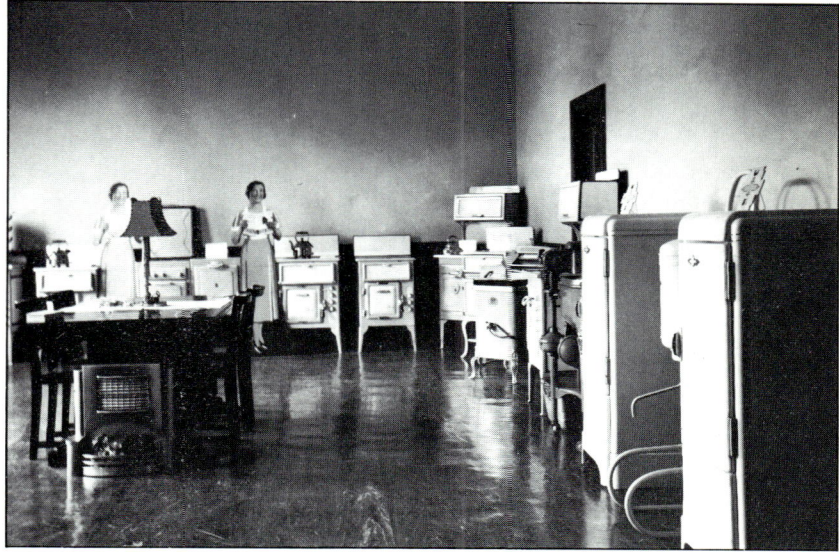

there was nothing to keep the cooker at the temperature you wanted either. These coal-fired cookers were made of black cast iron. To keep them a nice shiny black, the conscientious housewife cleaned them every day with black lead. So it's no wonder the cardboard housewife is smiling.

The fridges on the right of the photograph did away with the need for separate larders, and the need to shop every day in summer. They kept food fresh and cool for days on end, and discouraged the flies.

HELP IN THE HOUSE

(Left) In the UK, with its tradition of domestic servants even in quite ordinary homes, labour-saving appliances did not catch on as quickly as in the United States. But as the choice of jobs for girls gradually widened, the supply of domestic servants dwindled. As a result, the number of domestic appliances in the shops increased, often imported from the US or adapted from successful American models.

This Columbus Dixon suction floor polisher made cleaning the lino much easier – no need to get down on hands and knees when the machine's rotating polishing heads will do the work for you.

A GAS COOKER

(Above) If you did not like cooking by electricity, you could always use gas if you lived in an urban area. This gas cooker looks as clumsy to us as its rivals in the electricity showroom above. The saucepans, too, are quite a different shape from ours today, and there were no bright colours either.

All these new appliances in the 1930s helped to change people's ideas about housework.

A TOYSHOP IN WARTIME

The magic of model trains works even in wartime, when everything is in short supply. The photograph above was taken in 1941, at the height of the Second World War.

These boys could not go into a toyshop and expect to see a huge range of toys. Metals and other materials were far too precious to use for making toys, and were needed for tanks and guns. In fact, if you look closely, there is very little choice here, and most of the train sets are identical. So, although the shop window looks quite full, it does not really have much to sell.

The engines are, of course, models of steam engines. Diesel locomotives were not yet used.

You can tell this photograph was taken during the Second World War because of what the boys are carrying slung over their shoulders. Those square things are not satchels or lunch-boxes, they are gas masks. Everyone was supposed to carry a gas mask in case of an enemy gas attack.

KARDOMAH CAFE

(Below) Even in wartime life goes on as normally as possible. As the sign says, it is 'Business as usual'. Shoppers and office workers still need somewhere to have lunch or a snack. So shops and restaurants keep going, even though some goods are in short supply and sandbags are piled against the shopfront to stop the blast from an exploding bomb blowing in the windows.

The Kardomah chain of inexpensive restaurants was one of many that grew up to cater for the growing number of office workers, many of them women.

NYLON STOCKINGS

(Above) If she needed proof that things were getting better after the end of the war (1945), this happy shopper found it in a London store in December 1946. She had queued outside Selfridges in Oxford Street since early morning to be sure of getting a pair of nylon stockings (tights have only been part of women's everyday clothes since the 1960s). Nylon stockings were something quite new in Britain – indeed nylon itself was a new invention, developed in the 1930s.

These stockings are not as fine as today's nylon tights, but from the expression on her face they are still luxury. Throughout the war years (1939-45) she, along with every other woman in Britain, had had to make do with thick 'sensible' stockings, darned and mended to make them last.

Look at her 'hat'. It may not be as glamorous as some of the others in the book, but it is much more practical. During the war more women than ever before worked in factories, replacing the men called up to join the armed forces. Most women, however, had fairly long hair styles which could be dangerous in a factory – getting caught in machinery, for example. To overcome the problem they wore their hair done up like this. Clementine Churchill, the wife of the Prime Minister, adopted the style as a gesture of support for the contribution women were making to the country's war effort.

1948

SELF-SERVICE

It is hard to believe that self-service shopping in Britain is less than 40 years old.

The shops on this page have bravely adopted the new style of shopping – removing the counter and letting the customers help themselves to what they want from the shelves. It meant that shopkeepers needed fewer assistants, but they did need people to keep the shelves filled up.

Although the Second World War ended in 1945, many goods were in short supply for a long time afterwards, and were rationed by the government to make sure everyone got their fair share. On the price cards in the top picture you can see the cost of each item in both money and points. Everyone was allocated a certain number of points per month which they could use on whatever foods they liked.

Some goods, however, such as the tea in the top picture, were on full ration. This meant that everyone had a fixed allowance which was all they were allowed to buy each month. Once they had used up their allowance, their ration, they could not buy any more.

Householders were issued with ration books, and also with points coupons, which the shopkeeper took at the same time as the money. The woman with glasses in the bottom picture is holding out her ration book.

Rationing did not finally end until 1955, although some things had come 'off ration' before that.

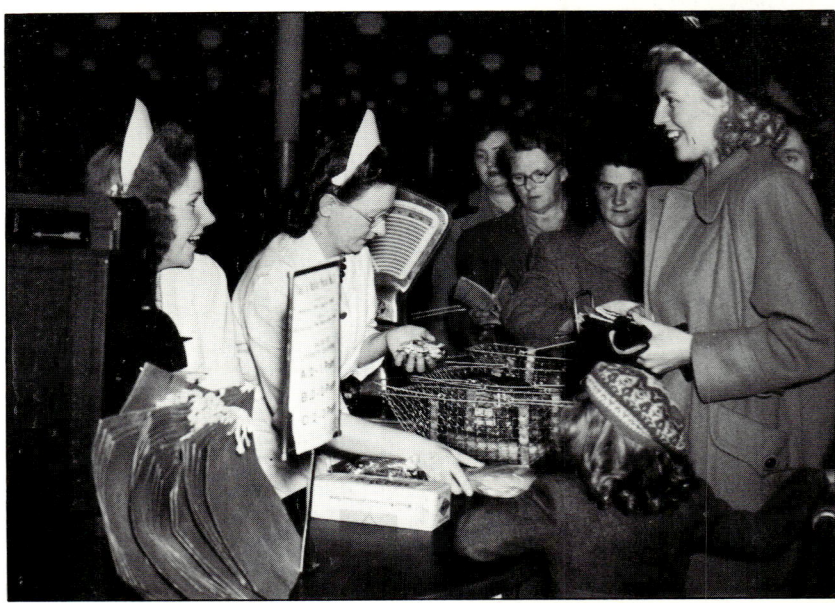

GENERAL STORE

The shop was often the hub of a village, providing much more than a place to buy food and drink.

Once a week this village shop at Chilham in Kent became the local library. The librarian came with a new stock of books, and borrowers did not have to go to a library in a distant town. Today travelling libraries have replaced this service, and Boots and W. H. Smith no longer have libraries of their own.

Food rationing, which continued after the war (see opposite), could help to explain the half-empty shelves here, and the limited range of goods on sale.

Some of these items (which ones?) are still available today, but many others are not. It would also be unusual today to find large cheeses like these Cheddars (bottom left) wrapped in traditional cheesecloth and stacked on the floor.

Notice the packaging. The cans on the left, for example, are particularly bare – a symptom again of postwar shortages.

A MODERN SUPERMARKET

And this is what we have today – shops of a size and with a range of goods undreamed of by the shoppers and shopkeepers in this book.

But how long will shopping remain like this? Already the big banks and store groups are discussing electronic shopping. You sit at home with your personal computer terminal, link it into a store's central ordering system, tap out details of what you want to buy; the money is automatically deducted from your account, and the goods are ready to collect when you arrive to pick them up – or are delivered to your door. That, at least, is the theory...

Time chart

1727 Sensitivity of silver salts to light discovered

1780 Browns of Chester opens

1790 Dickins & Smith (later Dickins & Jones) opens in London

1796 J. Watts, draper, opens in Manchester, becoming in 1836 Kendal Milne & Faulkener

1800 Tom Wedgwood makes 'sun' pictures by placing leaves on specially treated leather and leaving them in the sun. The parts covered by the leaves did not darken like the rest and when they were removed their image remained on the leather

1810 John Harris Heal opens his furniture shop in London

1812 John Swan and William Edgar open their shop in Piccadilly, London

1813 The building of Regent Street, London, begins

1836 Queen Victoria comes to the throne

1842 Beecham's pills first sold in Wigan market
Maples furniture store opens in Tottenham Court Road, London
Lilley & Skinner founded. Later in the nineteenth century they became pioneers in the mass production of machine-made shoes

1844 First successful Co-op starts in Rochdale

1849 Henry Charles Harrod opens his grocery shop in Brompton Road, London

1855 Roger Fenton takes documentary photographs of the Crimean War

1856 Singer Sewing Machine company opens its first shop, in Glasgow

1859 First advertisement for Beecham's pills appears

1864 John Lewis opens his shop in London's Oxford Street

1869 First Sainsbury grocery shop opens

1879 Passenger lifts installed in the Army and Navy Stores, London – probably the first in a department store (or any other shop) in the country

1880 First ever cargo of frozen meat arrives from Australia
Lewis's, Manchester, opens

1882 Fenwicks open in Newcastle

1884 Michael Marks sets up his first stall in Leeds market with the slogan 'Don't ask the price, it's a penny'

*1888 The first Kodak camera produced
Kodak processing service set up by George Eastman*

1891 Harrods install an escalator, the first in Britain

1892 Cine film perfected
Michael Marks opens his first high street shop in Manchester – before this the business had been in market stalls and covered markets

1894 Thomas Spencer joins Michael Marks

*c.*1900 The first electric till introduced

1901 Queen Victoria dies and Edward VII comes to the throne

1907 Autochrome, the first practical system of colour photography, goes on sale

1909 Woolworths open in England
Gordon Selfridge opens his store in Oxford Street, London

1910 Edward VII dies and George V comes to the throne

1914 First World War begins

1918 First World War ends

1926 Beecham's powders go on sale

1929 Flashbulbs for cameras introduced, enabling pictures to be taken in bad light

*c.*1931 John Cohen opens his first Tesco shop

1936 George V dies and George VI comes to the throne
Kodachrome, the first modern film, goes on sale. In an improved version it is still used for slides

1939 Second World War begins

1940 Butter, bacon and sugar are rationed
The importing of bananas is stopped

1945 Second World War ends

1946 Bread goes on ration – there was a worldwide shortage of grain for flour

1947 'Instant' Polaroid cameras go on sale
Self-service introduced

*c.*1950 Marks and Spencer open their first self-service food department

1952 George VI dies and Elizabeth II comes to the throne
Rationing of most goods comes to an end

1963 Polaroid colour cameras go on sale
Kodak introduce the first 'Instamatic' pocket camera

1969 First photographs taken on the moon

The entries in *italics* refer to the development of photography.

45

Things to do

PRICES AND CURRENCY

Shopping, of course, is about spending money. But although you will see prices mentioned in this book, it is really impossible to compare prices because the value of money has changed so much. Today's average *weekly* wage of around £150 is more than many people in this book earned in a whole year.

The system of money we use now is also quite different from that used throughout the period covered by this book. The decimal system, introduced in 1971, uses only pence and pounds. Before that there were pence, shillings and pounds.

The old system worked like this: 12 pence = 1 shilling; 20 shillings = £1. There were 240 of the old pence in one pound, not 100 as now. This means that every new penny is worth nearly 2½ old pence. One shilling is now 5 pence, two shillings is 10 pence, and so on. In the changeover to decimal currency, the only thing that kept the same value was the pound.

The old currency was written in a different way too, of course. The sum of 5 shillings and 11 pence (nearly 30 new pence) was usually written 5/11d, or sometimes just 5/11. The 'd' is the old symbol for a penny (and came from the latin *denarius*, which was a small coin).

Go through the book making a note of the prices charged for different goods, and also the date. Convert the prices to modern currency, and compare them with each other and with today. What can you learn from this? (You will have to look carefully sometimes to see all the prices.)

COINS AND NOTES

Today we have eight different coins, although the ½p is being phased out. Shoppers in Victorian times had many more coins, but notes were rare. The lowest value note was £5, which was a tremendous amount of money, probably nearer £50 today.

Find out what all the old coins were, the value of each one, and when they were withdrawn from circulation (if they were). Find pictures or draw examples of each coin to scale.

DEPARTMENT STORES

What is your nearest department store? Find out as much as you can about it and then write its history.

Among the things you will need to find out are: who started it and when, what it sold when it first opened, when it expanded and started selling other goods, whether it was always on that site, whether it is independent or part of a larger group. Other interesting points are whether it was built with lifts and escalators or had to install them in an existing building, when it first opened a restaurant and/or a coffee shop, and, if it is an old and long-established store, when it held its first sale.

The local Chamber of Commerce, library and newspaper are all good sources of information.

PACKAGING

Choose a well-known brand of food, but not something that has been introduced recently, and trace the changes in the way it has been packaged since it was introduced. The wrapping may have changed from paper to plastic, or glass to polythene, the shape of the container may have altered, the lettering and colour scheme may also have changed, sometimes more than once. Most manufacturers are generally helpful, and some of the larger ones have information packs for schools.

A PHOTO ESSAY

Make a photographic record of your local high street. Don't just photograph the shop windows, stand on the opposite side of the street and photograph the buildings above the shops as well.

This may give you a few surprises. For example, many quite modern-looking shops are actually single-storey buildings added onto the front of much older buildings.

Try and identify the approximate date of the original buildings from the style of architecture. Sometimes, if you are lucky, there will be a date on the building, where some proud shopkeeper has had inset the date he opened his shop on that site.

The National Trust Book of the English Country Town by Russell Chamberlain (Webb and Bower)
Market Towns of England by Garry Hogg (David & Charles)
Two books which, though they do not deal specifically with shops and shopping, have many fine pictures of some of the country's loveliest old towns. The photographs will also help you identify different styles of architecture.

Life in Edwardian England by Robert Cecil (B.T. Batsford)
An overall look at the period, which also includes information on the development of towns and other social changes which affected shops and shopping.

Victorian London by Priscilla Metcalf (Cassell)
A lively illustrated history of Queen Victoria's capital city, which includes the changes and developments in shopping habits.

Victorian and Edwardian Birmingham by D. McCulla (B.T. Batsford)
Victorian and Edwardian Brighton by John Betjeman and J.S. Gray (B.T. Batsford)
Victorian and Edwardian Bristol by Reece Winstone (B.T. Batsford)
Victorian and Edwardian Manchester by George Chandler (B.T. Batsford)
Victorian and Edwardian Liverpool and the North-west by George Chandler (B.T. Batsford)
Collections of early photographs which show different aspects of life in the different cities; there are many views of old shopping streets and markets.

A History of Regent Street by Hermione Hobhouse (Thames & Hudson)
A history of one of the world's most famous shopping streets, which from its very beginning was designed for shopkeepers and their customers.

Shopping in Style, London from Restoration to Edwardian Elegance by Alison Adburgham (Thames & Hudson)
The development of London as a shopping centre, mainly through the eyes of the rich and fashionable.

Shops and Shopping 1800-1914 by Alison Adburgham (Allen & Unwin)
Although concentrating on London and the well-to-do shopper, there is also quite a lot of information about the growth of shopping in the provinces and the rapidly growing industrial cities of England.

Edwardian Shopping, edited by J. Langbridge (David & Charles)
These selections from the Army and Navy Stores' catalogue are fascinating to 'dip' into, and reveal a lot about the Edwardian way of life. It's surprising the things they thought quite essential.

Your local library and county records office are probably also good sources of local information, and may even have published booklets about your area. Many of them will also have collections of old photographs which you can see on application.

Index

48